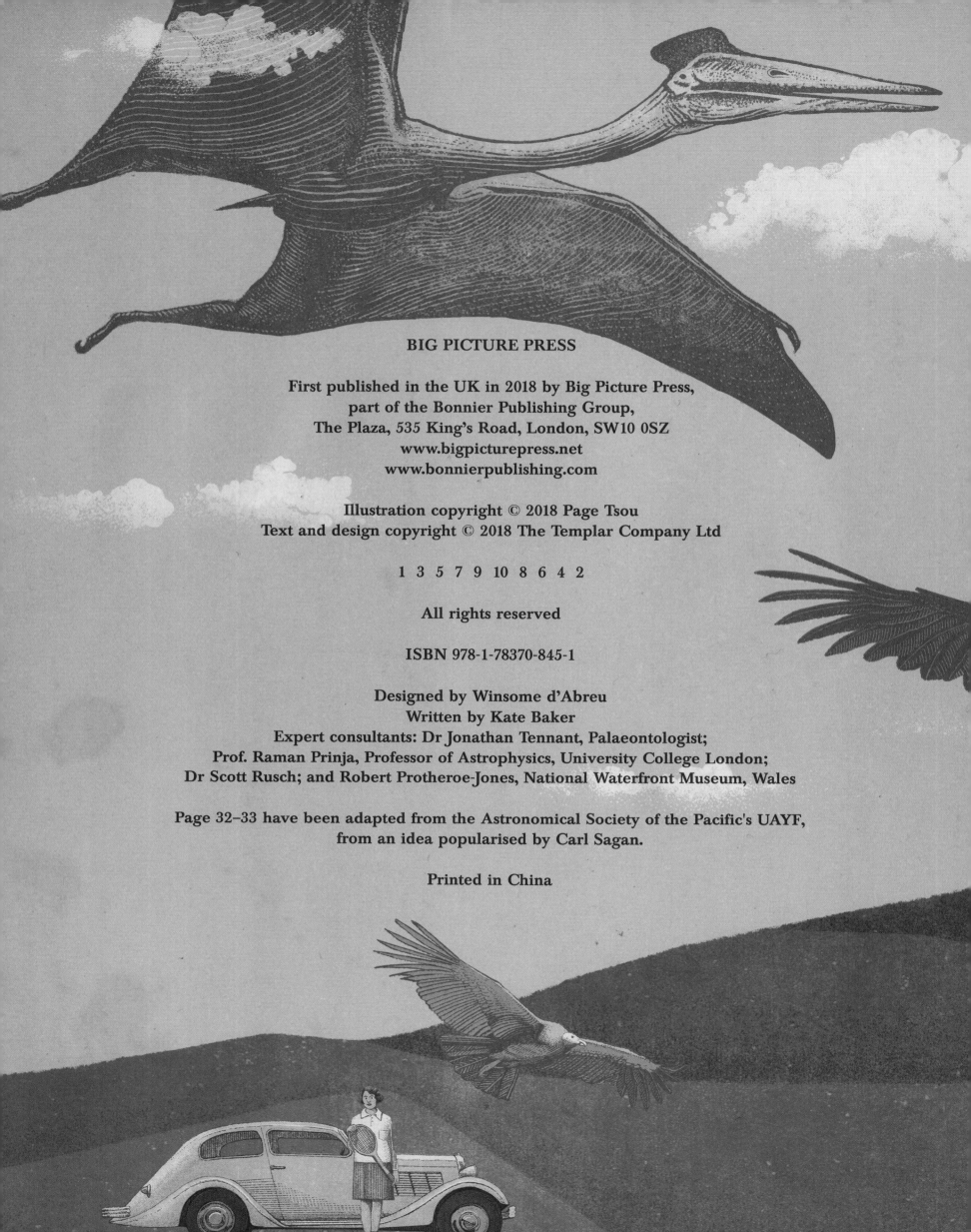

BIG PICTURE PRESS

First published in the UK in 2018 by Big Picture Press,
part of the Bonnier Publishing Group,
The Plaza, 535 King's Road, London, SW10 0SZ
www.bigpicturepress.net
www.bonnierpublishing.com

1 3 5 7 9 10 8 6 4 2

ISBN 978-1-78370-845-1

Designed by Winsome d'Abreu
Written by Kate Baker
Expert consultants: Dr Jonathan Tennant, Palaeontologist;
Prof. Raman Prinja, Professor of Astrophysics, University College London;
Dr Scott Rusch; and Robert Protheroe-Jones, National Waterfront Museum, Wales

Page 32–33 have been adapted from the Astronomical Society of the Pacific's UAYF,
from an idea popularised by Carl Sagan.

Printed in China

TALLEST TOWER SMALLEST STAR

A PICTORIAL COMPENDIUM OF COMPARISONS

ILLUSTRATED BY PAGE TSOU

B P P

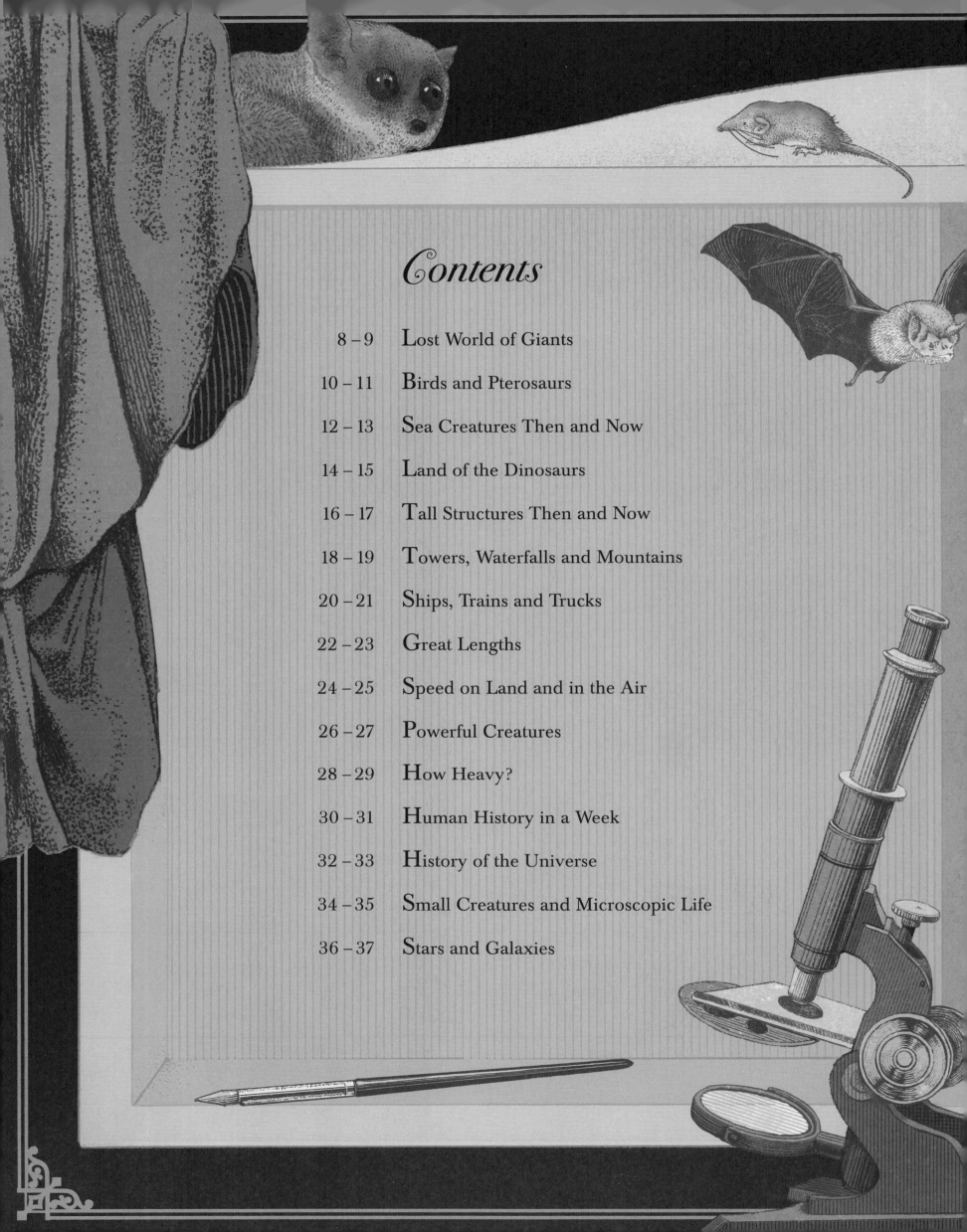

Contents

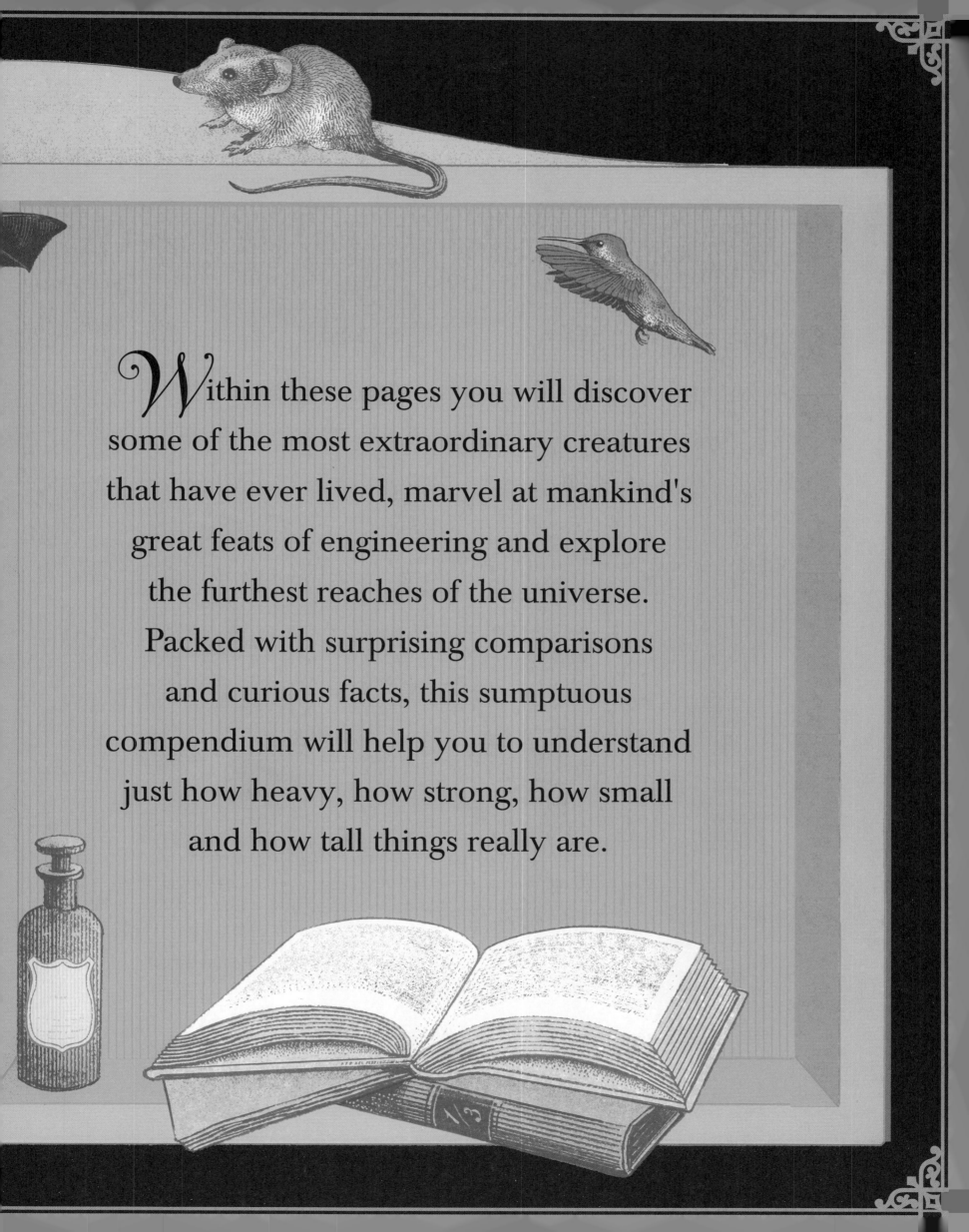

Within these pages you will discover some of the most extraordinary creatures that have ever lived, marvel at mankind's great feats of engineering and explore the furthest reaches of the universe. Packed with surprising comparisons and curious facts, this sumptuous compendium will help you to understand just how heavy, how strong, how small and how tall things really are.

Lost World OF Giants

Fossil discoveries have revealed an amazing world of extinct megafauna – enormous versions of creatures that live today. Imagine beavers the size of bears, sloths as large as elephants and armadillos as big as a car. Many of these creatures lived alongside early humans and their cousins, and may have either hunted them or been hunted by them. Most megafauna species died out due to dramatic climate changes around the end of the last Ice Age 11,700 years ago.

CREATURES THEN

❶ *Hyracotherium*
Shoulder height: 30–60 cm | Weight: 9 kg
Lived: Europe, N. America, c.55–33 mya
Not all prehistoric creatures were bigger than they are today. This early horse was around the same size as a small dog.

❷ *Mammuthus primigenius*
Height: 3–3.5 m | Weight: 6.6 tonnes
Lived: Asia, Europe, N. America, c.700,000–4,000 ya
The 'woolly mammoth' was similar in size to the average elephant. Unlike its modern relative, it had a coat of thick, curly fur to keep it warm in the cold temperatures, and long, twisted tusks that could grow more than 4 metres long. It was once thought that the mummified remains of mammoths discovered in the Siberian permafrost belonged to giant burrowing animals that died as soon as they were exposed to sunlight.

❸ *Titanoboa cerrejonensis*
Length: 13–14.6 m | Weight: 1 tonne
Lived: S. America, c.60–58 mya
These monstrous snakes lived in the rainforests of South America millions of years ago. They were longer than a bus and were capable of swallowing a crocodile whole.

❹ *Paraceratherium*
Shoulder height: 5.5 m (up to 8 m with its head raised) | Weight: 15–20 tonnes
Lived: Europe and Asia, c.30–16.6 mya
This enormous plant-eating rhinoceros was perhaps the largest land mammal of all time. With its head raised it stood around two times taller than an elephant. It used its long, thick neck to reach leaves high in the treetops.

❺ *Castoroides*
Length: 2.5 m | Weight: 125 kg | Lived: N. America, c.1.4 mya–10,000 ya
These bear-sized beavers had cutting teeth that could grow up to 15 cm long.

❻ *Megalania prisca*
Length: 5.5 m | Weight: 600 kg
Lived: Australia, c.1.8 mya–40,000 ya
Fossil finds suggest that this terrifying ancient lizard feasted on komodo dragons and giant kangaroos. It is thought that – as well as having very sharp teeth – it had toxic saliva that sen its victims into shock.

❼ *Glyptodon clavipes*
Length: 3.3 m | Weight: 2 tonnes
Lived: S. and N. America, c.5.3 mya–11,700 ya
This huge armadillo was roughly the same size and shape as a Volkswagen Beetle car. It was armed with a thick,

id shell and a powerful spiked tail
at it could swing like a baseball bat.
get past the *Glyptodon*'s armour to its
ft belly, predators would have needed
flip it over onto its back – no easy task
ven that it weighed up to 2 tonnes!

Megatherium americanum
ength: 6 m | Weight: 3.8 tonnes
ved: S. America, c.1.8 mya–10,000 ya
is mega-sized sloth usually walked
all fours, but its fossilized footprints
ow that it could also walk on two legs
short distances, leaving its arms and
ws free to grab twigs and leaves.
hen standing upright it would have
en as tall as a two-storey house.

CREATURES NOW

A. *Equus ferus caballus* (Horse)
Shoulder height: 1.7 m | Weight: 900 kg
Lives: Worldwide, except polar regions

**B. *Loxodonta africana*
(African elephant)**
Height: 4 m | Weight: 6.3 tonnes
Lives: Africa, Asia
Elephants are the biggest and heaviest
land creatures alive today.

**C. *Boa constrictor*
(Boa constrictor)**
Length: 4 m | Weight: 45 kg
Lives: Central and S. America

**D. *Rhinocerotidae*
(White rhinoceros)**
Shoulder height: 2 m | Weight: 3.6
tonnes | Lives: Africa, Asia

**E. *Castor canadensis*
(American beaver)**
Length (not including tail): 0.9 m
Weight: 32 kg | Lives: N. America

**F. *Varanus niloticus*
(Nile monitor lizard)** | Length:
2.4 m | Weight: 15 kg | Lives: Africa

**G. *Priodontes maximus*
(Giant armadillo)**
Length (not including tail): 1 m
Weight: 32 kg | Lives: S. America

**H. *Choloepus hoffmanni*
(Hoffman's Two-Toed Sloth)**
Height: 74 cm | Weight: 9 kg
Lives: Central and S. America

ya = years ago
mya = million years ago
Megafauna – The term megafauna is
used to describe large ('mega') animals
('fauna') with an adult body weight
of over 45 kg. Humans are actually
megafauna, as are elephants, giraffes,
whales and lions.

Birds Today

A. *Diomedea exulans* (**Wandering albatross**)
Wingspan: 3.5 m | Lives: Southern Hemisphere
Has the longest wingspan of any living bird

B. *Vultur gryphus* (**Andean condor**)
Wingspan: 3.2 m | Lives: S. America

C. *Aquila chrysaetos* (**Golden eagle**) | Wingspan: 2.3 m
Lives: Africa, Asia, C. and N. America, Europe

D. *Pica pica* (**Common magpie**)
Wingspan: 57 cm | Lives: Africa, Asia, Europe

E. *Apteryx* (**Kiwi**)
Length: 45 cm | Lives: New Zealand
The closest living relative of the elephant bird

F. *Struthio camelus* (**Common ostrich**)
Height: 2.8 m | Lives: Africa
The largest bird alive today

G. *Caloenas nicobarica* (**Nicobar pigeon**)
Length: 40 cm | Lives: Asia and the Pacific
The dodo's closest living relative

BIRDS & PTEROSAURS

During the time of the dinosaurs the skies were ruled by flying reptiles known as pterosaurs. Some were small enough to fit in the palm of a hand, but one of the largest – the *Quetzalcoatlus* – was as tall as a giraffe and had wings as big as a spitfire plane. The pterosaurs died out around 66 million years ago, making way for another group of flying animals – birds. Over millions of years birds have evolved into an array of shapes, colours and sizes, but none have ever reached the enormous size of the biggest pterosaurs.

Flying Things Then

❶ *Quetzalcoatlus northropi*
Wingspan: 10–11 m | Lived: America, c.68–66 mya
When the fossilized remains of this giraffe-sized pterosaur were found in the American desert, people marvelled that creatures that large could fly. Its secret lay in its hollow arm bones, which made it very lightweight. It also kept its wing beats to a minimum and used its wings of toughened skin to glide great distances. It was probably a scavenger and used its long neck to reach into the carcasses of dead dinosaurs.

❷ *Pelagornis sandersi*
Wingspan: 6.1–7.4 m | Lived: N. America, c.28–25 mya
This enormous seabird glided over ancient oceans millions of years ago. With a wingspan longer than a stretch limousine, it competes with the *Argentavis magnificens* for the title of largest flying bird of all time.

❸ *Argentavis magnificens*
Wingspan: 6.5–7.5 m | Lived: S. America, c.6 mya
This huge bird is an ancestor of the giant condor.

❹ *Archaeopteryx lithographica* – 'The first bird'
Height: 0.3 m | Lived: Europe, c.150 mya
Birds did not evolve from pterosaurs but from small, meat-eating dinosaurs. The magpie-sized *Archaeopteryx* is often thought of as the 'missing link' between dinosaurs and birds. It was a primitive bird with feathers, but unlike modern birds it had a long tail and a full set of teeth. It is likely that it could fly at least short distances.

❺ *Harpagornis moorei* or 'Haast's eagle'
Wingspan: 3 m | Lived: New Zealand, c.1.8 mya– AD 1400 • One of the largest eagles that ever existed.

Flightless Birds Then

❻ *Dinornis robustus* or 'giant moa'
Height: Up to 3.6 m | Lived: New Zealand, c.8.5 mya– AD 1450 • The giant moa was one of the biggest flightless birds to have ever lived. They had large legs, but no wings, and were hunted to extinction by Maori settlers, who ate their meat and used their skin, feathers and bones to make clothes, fish hooks and pendants.

❼ *Aepyornis maximus* or 'elephant bird'
Height: 3 m | Lived: Madagascar, c.2 mya–AD 1650
Hundreds of years ago, adventurer Marco Polo came back from his adventures with stories of a bird so big that it could swoop down to snatch an elephant in its talons and fly through the air with it. In truth, the 'elephant bird' was a herbivore and it was flightless.

❽ *Titanis walleri*
Height: 2.5–3 m | Lived: N. America, c.4.9–1.8 mya
One of the last of the 'terror birds', the *titanis* was one of the top predators of its day. One theory is that it pinned prey to the ground with its claws, then swung its massive hooked beak at the creature like a pickaxe.

❾ *Raphus cucullatus* or 'dodo'
Height: up to 1 m | Lived: Mauritius, until c.AD 1662
These clumsy flightless birds lived and nested on the ground. They were discovered in the 1500s by Dutch explorers and around 100 years later they were extinct. Many had been eaten by the settlers, while their eggs had been eaten by pigs, cats and other animals that had been introduced to the island.

Sea Creatures Then and Now

For hundreds of years people have told tales of colossal sea creatures that could tear apart ships and drag sailors to a watery grave. Step back in time millions of years and the oceans were home to real live monsters – fearsome predatory whales, giant crocodiles and mega-toothed sharks that were three times the size of a great white shark. The largest animal ever to have lived – the blue whale – still lives in our oceans today. Despite its size, it is harmless to humans and lives on a diet of tiny crustaceans.

SEA CREATURES THEN

❶ Livyatan melvillei

Length: 18 m | Lived: S. America, c.13–12 mya
Named after the Biblical sea monster and
Herman Melville, the author of *Moby Dick*, this
predatory whale had gigantic teeth more than
36 cm long. It is thought that it patrolled the
world's oceans feasting on baleen whales.

❷ Basilosaurus isis (meaning 'king lizard')

Length: 18 m | Lived: N. Africa, N. America
and Asia, c.40–30 mya
Despite their name, these fearsome predators
were not reptiles – they were enormous,
ancient whales. They had long snakelike bodies
and a powerful bite capable of crunching

through bones. There is evidence that, like
modern killer whales, they even preyed on
other whales.

❸ Carcharocles megalodon
(meaning 'megatooth')

Length: 18 m | Lived: Oceans around the
world, c.15.9–2.6 mya
These colossal sharks were around three times
longer than a great white, and their jaws were
2.7 m tall – big enough to swallow a human
whole. A single *Megalodon* tooth was more than
16 cm long and was used to tear into the flesh
and crush the bones of other sea animals.
Many years ago, fossilised shark teeth, found
washed up on the shore, were thought to be
the petrified tongues of dragons or snakes.

❹ Shonisaurus sikanniensis sp.
(meaning 'lizard from the Shoshone Mountains')

Length: 21 m | Lived: N. America, c.220 mya
One of the largest marine reptiles that has yet
been found, the *Shonisaurus* was longer than
most modern whales. It had a short, toothless
snout and is thought to have been a filter-
feeder, sucking in food through its open jaws.

❺ Machimosaurus rex
(meaning 'fighting lizard-king')

Length: 10 m | Lived: Africa, c.132–129 mya
This ancient crocodile ancestor was as long as
a bus and its skull alone was as long as person
is tall. Its massive jaws were filled with sharp
bullet-shaped teeth that it used to crunch
through the shells of turtles.

SEA CREATURES NOW

A. Balaenoptera musculus
(Blue whale)

Length: 32 m | Lives: All oceans except
enclosed seas and the Arctic
Bigger than any dinosaur, the blue whale is as
long as a Boeing 737 plane.

B. Carcharodon carcharias
(Great white shark)

Length: 6 m | Lives: Oceans around the world

C. Crocodylus porosus
(Saltwater crocodile)

Length: 5.48 m | Lives: Indian, Pacific oceans

Land of the Dinosaurs

For over 160 million years, dinosaurs dominated our planet. They came in many different forms – from giant, peaceful plant-eaters to sturdy armoured stegosaurs and carnivorous theropods. Many of them would have towered over even the biggest creatures alive today. Others were surprisingly small – like the chicken-sized *Compsognathus*.

DINOSAURS CAN BE GROUPED INTO THREE MAIN TYPES:

Theropods – *mostly meat-eaters with powerful legs and short arms*
Ornithischians – *bird-hipped, herbivorous and often armoured dinosaurs*
Sauropods – *herbivores with long necks and tails; walked on four feet*

Tyrannosaurus rex
A fierce hunter and scavenger, and one of the most famous of the theropods
TYPE: **Theropod**
LENGTH: 12.3 m
HEIGHT: 5 m

Sauroposeidon proteles
TYPE: **Sauropod**
LENGTH: 34 m
HEIGHT: 18 m
Thought to be the tallest dinosaur to have ever walked the Earth, this massive herbivore was bigger than a six-storey building and had legs as thick as tree trunks. Despite its size, its head was around the same size as that of a horse.

Triceratops horridus – A four-legged ceratopsian dinosaur with three horns and a bony frill
TYPE: **Ornithischian**
LENGTH: 8–9 m
HEIGHT: 3 m (top of head)

Stegosaurus stenops – The most famous of the stegosaurs, a group of slow-moving, plant-eating dinosaurs with bony plates or spikes on their backs
TYPE: **Ornithischian**
LENGTH: 9 m
HEIGHT: 3.5 m
PLATES: 60 cm wide and tall

Iguanodon bernissartensis
An example of an ornithopod dinosaur, which walked and ran on two back feet
TYPE: **Ornithischian**
LENGTH: 10–13 m
HEIGHT: 3.3 m

Looking at the Evidence

GIANT BONES

Measuring as much as 2.4 m, the thigh bone of the monster-sized *Titanosaur* is bigger than a fully grown person.

DINOSAUR TEETH

Dinosaur teeth hold many clues about what and how these creatures ate. The meat-eating *Tyrannosaurus* had teeth as long as bread knives and its bite was at least three times as powerful as that of a lion. The plant-eating triceratops, meanwhile, may have had as many as 800 teeth, stacked in columns, although only a small number of these were in use at any one time.

1. *Spinosaurus*
22.5 cm
Long and spear-like, for catching fish

2. *Tyrannosaurus*
20 cm
Had serrated edges for tearing flesh and crunching bones

3. *Diplodocus*
8 cm
Narrow and peglike, for stripping leaves from trees and raking through vegetation

4. *Triceratops*
5 cm
Used for shearing vegetation

5. Lion
10 cm

6. Human
1.25 cm

MONSTER EGGS

The smallest dinosaur eggs were the size of tennis balls; the biggest were like giant footballs. Compared to their enormous size, the mighty sauropods laid surprisingly small eggs – in fact, not much larger than an ostrich's egg. Scientists think that these smaller eggs may have taken less time to hatch and so reduced the risk of them being eaten by predators.

1. Chicken egg – 5.7 cm

2. Ostrich egg – 15 cm

3. *Titanosaur* (sauropod) egg – 22 cm

How Big?

See how these different giants measured up...

20 m
18 m
16 m
14 m
12 m
10 m
8 m
6 m
4 m

Triceratops   *Iguanodon*   *Stegosaurus*   *Diplodocus*   Giraffe   *Tyrannosaurus*   Man   *Spinosaurus*   *Sauroposeidon*

TALL STRUCTURES *Then & Now*

Dinosaurs may have been the tallest creatures ever to have roamed the Earth, but they look mouse-like when compared to some of the great buildings of the world. Throughout history, man has built some extraordinary structures – from the mysterious columns of Stonehenge to the white marble domes of the Taj Mahal. Dwarfing them all for around 3,800 years was the Great Pyramid of Giza – a glittering monument to the mighty Ancient Egyptian civilization.

❶ 10 m – Stonehenge, Wiltshire, England, c.2500 BC

❷ 12 m – Statue of Zeus, Olympia, Greece, c.430 BC *

❸ 18 m – Temple of Artemis, Ephesus, Turkey, c.550 BC; rebuilt in c.356 BC *

❹ 21 m – Cleopatra's Needle, Heliopolis, Egypt, c.1460 BC, now located in London, England

❺ 24 m – El Castillo, Chichén Itzá, Mexico, c.AD 1000–1200

❻ 32 m – Colossus of Rhodes, Rhodes, Greece, c.294–282 BC *

❼ 38 m – Christ the Redeemer, Rio de Janeiro, Brazil, AD 1931 (height includes the pedestal)

❽ 48 m – Colosseum, Rome, Italy, AD 80

❾ 50 m – Arc de Triomphe, Paris, France, AD 1836

❿ 55.7 m – Leaning Tower of Pisa, Pisa, Italy, AD 1360

⓫ 57 m – St Basil's Cathedral, Moscow, Russia, AD 1554–1560

⓬ 60 m – Big Wild Goose Pagoda, Shaanxi province, China, AD 652

⓭ 73 m – Taj Mahal, Agra, India, AD 1653

⓮ 93 m – Statue of Liberty, New York, USA, AD 1886 (height includes the pedestal)

⓯ 110 m – Lighthouse of Alexandria, Egypt, c.280 BC (the tallest lighthouse ever built) *

⓰ 111.3 m – St Paul's Cathedral, London, England, AD 1711

⓱ 132.5 m – St Peter's Basilica, Rome, Italy, AD 1626

⓲ 138.8 m – Great Pyramid of Giza, Cairo, Egypt, c.2560 BC (the only surviving Ancient Wonder, and the tallest man-made structure in the world for about 3,800 years; when built it stood 146.5 m tall) *

⓳ 169.1 m – Washington Monument, Washington, D.C., USA, AD 1884 (the world's tallest structure from AD 1884–1889)

* Ancient Wonders of the World

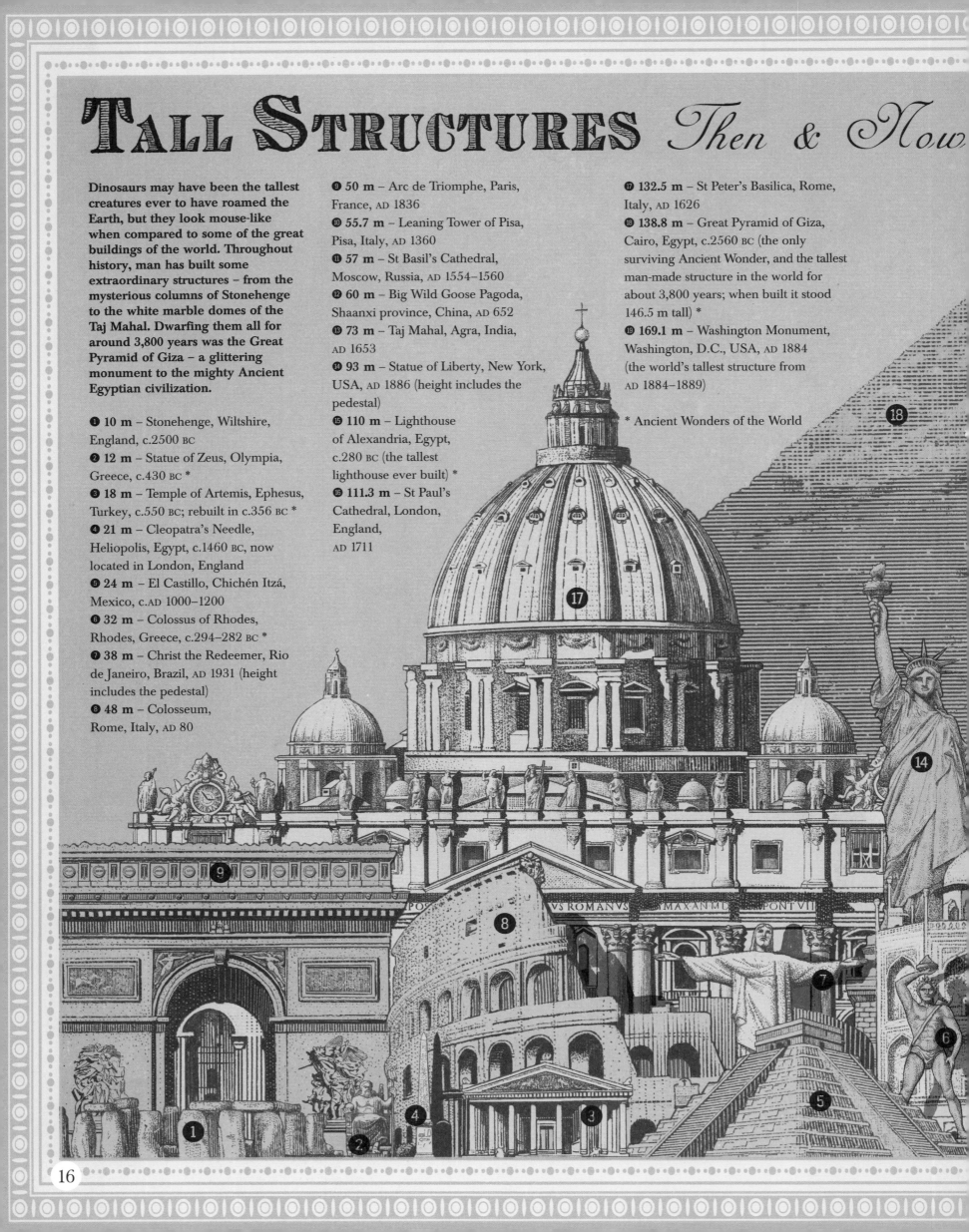

The Jewel of the Nile

Rising out of the deserts of Egypt, the Great Pyramid of Giza was once covered with highly polished limestone blocks. As the sunlight reflected on the pyramid's white surface it glistened like a jewel.

Thousands of workers, craftsmen and artisans were used to build the pyramid and it is estimated that it consists of around 2.3 million stone blocks.

Skyscrapers of the Future

Soaring skywards, far above the wonders of the ancient world, is Dubai's needle-shaped Burj Khalifa. At a dizzying 828 m, it is the same height as around 488 people, or 45 *Sauroposeidon* dinosaurs stacked on top of one another.

Today's record-holder will soon be surpassed by even taller buildings. The Jeddah Tower, under construction in Jeddah, Saudi Arabia, is set to reach a height of around 1,000 m.

170 m —
160 m —
150 m —
140 m —
130 m —
120 m —
110 m —
100 m —
90 m —
80 m —
70 m —
60 m —
50 m —
40 m —
30 m —
20 m —
10 m —

— 800m
— 700 m
— 600 m
— 500 m
— 400 m
— 300 m
— 200 m
— 100 m

THE TALLEST STRUCTURE EVER BUILT

828m
Burj Khalifa, Dubai, UAE, 2010 (world's tallest structure to date)

324m
Eiffel Tower, Paris, France, 1889 (held the record of the world's tallest structure from 1889–1930)

Towers, Waterfalls AND Mountains

**1,000 m
Jeddah Tower,
Jeddah, Saudi
Arabia (under
construction)**

1,000 m

900 m

800 m

700 m

600 m

500 m

400 m

300 m

200 m

100 m

Towers AND Waterfalls

Peeping through the clouds, hundreds of metres above the streets below, skyscrapers dominate the skyline of cities around the world. Rising higher still, is the magnificent Angel Falls. Hidden deep in the jungle of Venezuela, shrouded in mist, this spectacular waterfall is one of the greatest natural wonders on Earth.

Towers
❶ **828 m** – Burj Khalifa, Dubai, UAE, 2010
The world's current tallest structure
❷ **632 m** – Shanghai Tower, Shanghai, China, 2015
❸ **601 m** – Makkah Royal Clock Tower, Mecca, Saudi Arabia, 2012
❹ **541 m** – One World Trade Center, New York, USA, 2014
❺ **508 m** – Taipei 101, Taipei, Taiwan, 2004

Waterfalls
❻ **979 m** – Angel Falls, Bolivar State, Venezuela
The world's highest uninterrupted waterfall

Rivers of Gold and Devil Spirits
In 1937, the aviator and adventurer Jimmy Angel crash-landed his 4-seater plane on a mountaintop. He was searching for a legendary river of gold, but what he discovered instead were the Angel Falls. The Falls were already well known to the local Pemón people as Kerepakupai-Meru, or 'waterfall of the deepest place'. The Pemón believed that it was home to devil spirits called *mawari*, who stole the souls of the living.

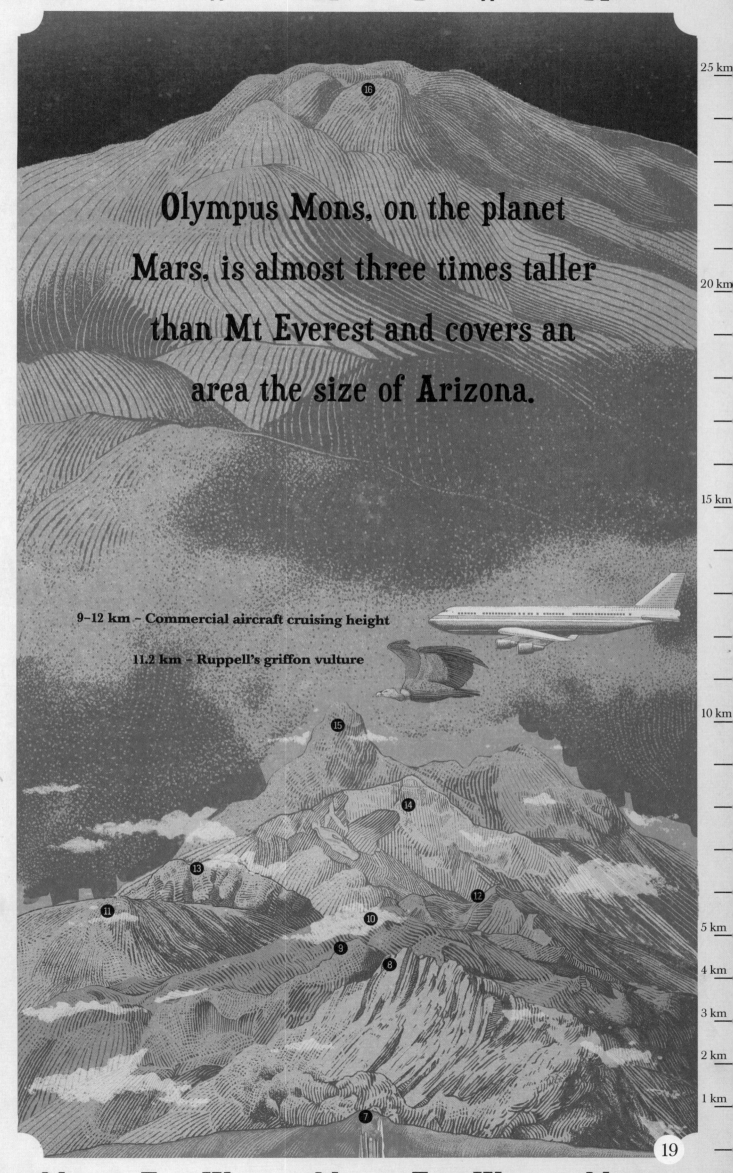

Mountains

The world's tallest towers and waterfalls pale in comparison with the largest mountains. Mt Everest is the same height as more than 10 Burj Khalifas stacked on top of one another. Yet even the mighty Himalayas look tiny compared to the highest mountain in our Solar System – Olympus Mons.

❼ 979 m – Angel Falls

Earth Mountains
❽ 4,884 m – Mt Puncak Jaya or Carstensz Pyramid
highest peak in Oceania
❾ 4,892 m – Mt Vinson
highest peak in Antarctica
❿ 5,642 m – Mt Elbrus
highest peak in Europe
⓫ 5,895 m – Mt Kilimanjaro
highest peak in Africa
⓬ 6,191 m – Mt Denali (also known as Mt McKinley)
highest peak in N. America
⓭ 6,961 m – Mt Aconcagua
highest peak in S. America
⓮ 8,848 m – Mt Everest
highest peak in Asia and highest mountain peak on Earth from sea level
⓯ 10,205 m – Mauna Kea, Hawaii, N. America
tallest mountain peak on Earth measured from its base

Although Mount Everest is the highest mountain on Earth measured from sea level, the tallest when measured from its base is in fact Mauna Kea. The peak of this million-year-old volcano rises 4,205 m from sea level, but its base plunges a further 6,000 m deep under the sea.

Tallest mountain in the Solar System
⓰ 25,000 m
Olympus Mons, Mars

Olympus Mons, on the planet Mars, is almost three times taller than Mt Everest and covers an area the size of Arizona.

9–12 km – **Commercial aircraft cruising height**

11.2 km – **Ruppell's griffon vulture**

25 km

20 km

15 km

10 km

5 km

4 km

3 km

2 km

1 km

SHIPS, TRAINS AND TRUCKS

Ships, trains and trucks are used around the globe to transport people and haul all kinds of things from gold and iron ore, food and coal, to cars, tanks, aircraft parts and even rubbish. They have allowed people to travel further and carry heavier loads than ever before, to explore new worlds and to discover treasures from distant lands.

SHIPS

SANTA MARIA
(1460)
TYPE: Carrack **COUNTRY**: Galicia
LENGTH: Estimated 30 m

Man in a canoe

The *Santa Maria* was the biggest of Christopher Columbus's three ships on his 1492 voyage to the 'New World'. It was designed for carrying lots of cargo and there were more than 40 men on board – including a carpenter, a painter, a goldsmith, a tailor and four known criminals.

CUTTY SARK
(1869)
TYPE: Clipper **COUNTRY**: UK
LENGTH: 64.8 m

Man in a canoe

Built to transport tea from China to London, this famous cargo ship could carry as many as 10,000 tea chests – enough for 200 million cups. As well as tea, she carried everything from coffee, coal, cocoa beans and beer, to wool, whale oil, shark bones, sardines and straw hats.

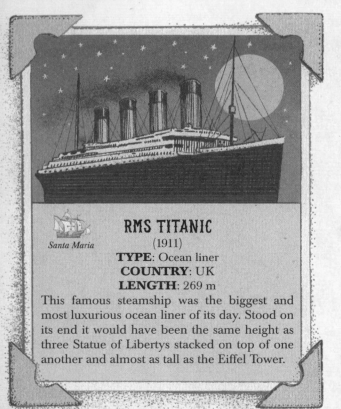

Santa Maria

RMS TITANIC
(1911)
TYPE: Ocean liner
COUNTRY: UK
LENGTH: 269 m

This famous steamship was the biggest and most luxurious ocean liner of its day. Stood on its end it would have been the same height as three Statue of Libertys stacked on top of one another and almost as tall as the Eiffel Tower.

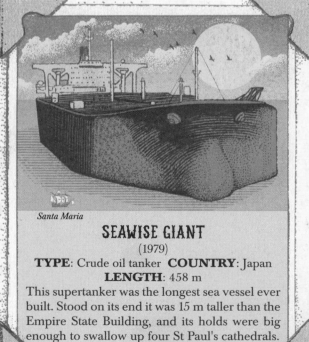

Santa Maria

SEAWISE GIANT
(1979)
TYPE: Crude oil tanker **COUNTRY**: Japan
LENGTH: 458 m

This supertanker was the longest sea vessel ever built. Stood on its end it was 15 m taller than the Empire State Building, and its holds were big enough to swallow up four St Paul's cathedrals.

BHP IRON ORE TRAIN
(2001)
TYPE: Freight train
COUNTRY: Australia
LENGTH: 7,353 m

Freight trains are some of the longest vehicles in the world. They use less fuel than trucks and are able to carry bigger loads over long distances. The biggest freight train of them all – the BHP iron ore train – was driven by eight locomotives and pulled 680 wagons across the Australian desert.

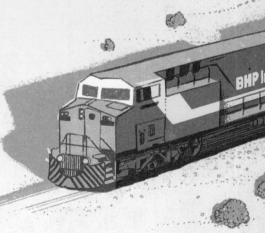

UNION PACIFIC 'BIG BOY'
(1941)
TYPE: Steam locomotive
COUNTRY: USA
LENGTH: 40.47 m (including the tender)

One of the largest steam locomotives ever built. In its heyday, this powerful engine pulled heavy freight trains over the mountains of Wyoming and Utah.

TRUCKS

BIG FOOT 5
(1986)
TYPE: Monster truck **COUNTRY**: USA
LENGTH: Around 6.5 m long, 4.7 m tall
Bigfoot 5 was the largest monster truck of all time. Its tyres alone stood 3 m tall. The hefty tyres once belonged to a US military vehicle called the Snow Train, which took supplies over deep snow to remote Arctic locations.

TRAINS

BELAZ 75710 MINING DUMP TRUCK
(2014)
TYPE: Haul truck **COUNTRY**: Belarus **LENGTH**: 20.6 m
The world's biggest mining truck hauls loads of metal ore weighing more than 40 tonnes from open cast mines. Temperatures in the mines can range from -50°C to +50°C.

PENYDARREN LOCOMOTIVE
(1804)
TYPE: Steam locomotive
COUNTRY: UK
LENGTH: 7.57 m (including the tender)
On 21 February 1804, Richard Trevithick's 'Penydarren' locomotive hauled five wagons loaded with 10 tonnes of iron ore and 70 people. It was the world's first-ever steam locomotive journey on rails.

AUSTRALIAN ROAD TRAIN
(2013)
TYPE: Heavy truck **COUNTRY**: Australia
LENGTH: 53m
Australian 'power trains' are some of the world's longest trucks. They are used to carry heavy goods like machinery, fuel, cattle or gold for thousands of kilometres across the Australian desert.

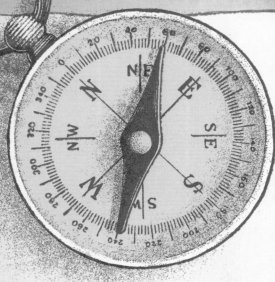

Great Lengths

Mountains and Reefs

Great Barrier Reef, Australia – 2,300 km
This natural wonder is the world's biggest reef and the largest living structure on the planet. Built over centuries by minuscule colonial animals called polyps, it is so big it can be seen from space. It is home to an extraordinary range of sea life, from tiny fish, to turtles, rays, sharks and whales.

Great Himalaya Range, Asia – 2,300 km
The Great Himalayas contains many of the biggest peaks on Earth, including the world's highest – Mt Everest. The mountains were formed some 70 million years ago when two massive tectonic plates collided. According to legends it is home to the yeti, a giant ape-like creature, and in Hindu mythology it is the home of the God Shiva.

The Andes Mountains, S. America – 8,900 km
The world's longest mountain chain was populated long ago by American Indian peoples, who farmed its steep slopes. Today about a third of all the people in South America live in the Andes. Its most famous animal inhabitants include llamas, alpacas, vicuñas, chinchillas and condors.

Rivers

Yangtze River, China – 6,300 km
The Yangtze River is the longest and busiest river in Asia. Along its course you will find some of the world's biggest cities, one of the deepest gorges (Tiger Leaping Gorge) and the world's biggest dam (Three Gorges Dam).

Amazon River, S. America – 6,400 km
The Amazon is one of the richest habitats on the planet. It is home to pink dolphins, anacondas, alligators, sloths and thousands of species of birds and fish. Around one in ten of all known species of wildlife live in the Amazon River Basin.

Nile River, Africa – 6,695 km
The longest river in the world, the Nile has been an important part of Egyptian life since ancient times. Each spring, the Nile floods, spreading fertile soil around its banks. This soil makes farming possible and brings life to the dry desert lands.

Mid-Ocean Ridge

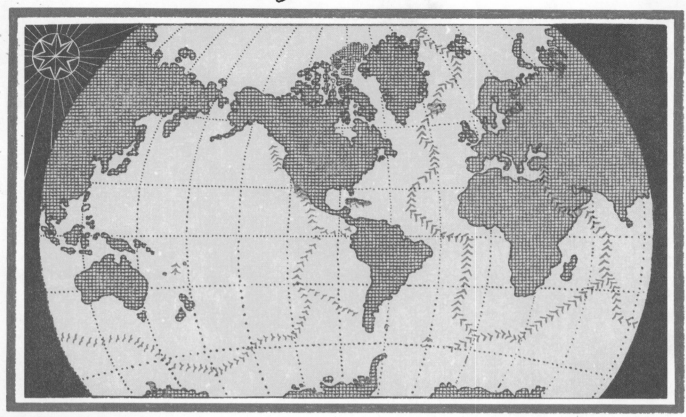

**Mid-Ocean Ridge –
60–65,000 km**
The longest and largest
mountain range on Earth
is in fact hidden from
view beneath the sea.
Starting in the Arctic
Ocean, the Mid-Ocean
Ridge system runs
through the Atlantic, past
Africa, Asia, Australia
and Antarctica, then
across the Pacific to
North America. With a
total length of around
65,000 km, it is more
than seven times
longer than the
longest ranges
on land.

0 ▬▬▬▬▬▬▬ 8,900 km
The Andes Mountains (the longest mountain range on land)

0 ▬▬▬▬▬▬▬▬▬▬▬▬▬▬▬▬▬▬▬▬▬▬▬▬▬▬ 65,000 km
Mid-Ocean Ridge (the longest mountain range under the sea)

Man-Made Structures

Trans-Siberian Railway (Moscow to Vladivostok)
Built: 21 July 1904 | Length – 9,258 km
One of the longest railways in the world, this famous route connects European
Russia with the Asian port of Vladivostok, near the border of China. Today, it
carries millions of passengers and about 100 million tonnes of freight each year.

Great Wall of China
Built c. 259 BC–AD 1644 | Length – 21,196 km
Built to keep northern invaders out of China, the Great Wall is the longest structure
ever constructed. It is thought that up to a million people died while building it, and it
has been discovered that the mortar used to bind the stones was made with sticky rice.

SPEED on Land and in the Air

Before the invention of planes, trains and flying machines, people travelled on land no faster than they could ride on a galloping horse. When the first steam trains were built, some feared it would be impossible to breathe while moving at such speed, or that the vibrations would be so powerful you might go blind. These fears were soon proved wrong and, ever since, people have strived to reach ever-greater speeds. On 26 May 1969, the Apollo 10 astronauts returning from their Moon mission zoomed to Earth at 39,937 kph – around twelve times faster than a rifle bullet and more than thirty times faster than the speed of sound.

FASTER THAN A SPACE SHUTTLE? When diving through the air, the tiny Anna's hummingbird can fly a mind-boggling 385 body lengths per second (blps). Relative to its size, that's even faster than a space shuttle on re-entry into the Earth's atmosphere (207 blps).

Apollo 10: 39,937 kph

North American X-15A2 (fastest non-space aircraft of all time, 3 October 1967): 7,270 kph

Commercial aircraft cruising speed: 920 kph

Westland Lynx (fastest helicopter,

Thrust SCC (the current holder of the official land-speed record, set in the Nevada Desert, USA in 1967): 1,227.98 kph

Bluebird CN7 car (broke the world land-speed record on 17 July 1964): 648.73 kph

Japanese LO Series maglev (fastest passenger train, 21 April 2015): 603 kph

LNER class A4 no.4468 Mallard (fastest steam train, 3 July 1938): 202 kph

... racing motorcar, 1904: 160 kph

Family car: 112 kph

Cheetah: 95 kph+

Although they can't fly, ostriches can run at speeds of around 72 kph – faster than a racehorse.

Stephenson's rocket, 1829: 45 kph

Benz Patent Motorwagon, 1885–1886 (the world's first automobile): 16 kph

... falcon (when diving): 250 kph

Spirit of St Louis (flown by Charles Lindbergh on the first solo transatlantic flight, in May 1927): 200 kph

Hindenburg zeppelin airship: 135 kph

On 19 September 1783, the Montgolfier brothers demonstrated their invention, the hot-air balloon, to a crowd of dignitaries. Its first passengers were a duck, a rooster and a sheep called Montauciel (meaning 'climb-to-the-sky'). The first manned flight travelled 9 km and took 25 minutes: around 20 kph.

Wright Flyer, 1903 (the world's first successful heavier-than-air flying machine): 15.58 kph

POWERFUL CREATURES

THE WORLD'S STRONGEST MEN

PULL

On 15 August 2016, Reverend Kevin Fast broke the world record by pulling a vehicle weighing 68,090 kg. That's around 400 times his body weight and equivalent to the combined weight of six buses (52,500 kg), four small family cars (4,000 kg) and one light aircraft (5,670 kg).

BACKLIFT

In 1957 it was claimed that Paul Anderson, one of the world's strongest men of all time, backlifted around 2,840 kg. That's the same weight as more than five polar bears.

DEADLIFT

The world's strongest man in 2016, Eddie Hall, deadlifted a 500 kg bar above his head – about the same weight as one polar bear or a large grand piano.

Mammals

For thousands of years, animals have been used for carrying or dragging heavy loads. They have ploughed fields, pulled wagons and carts, and transported people across deserts and mountains. But, when it comes to brute strength, the African elephant is the strongest of all land animals. A large bull elephant can carry as much as 9,000 kg – the same weight as around 140 people – and is able to lift logs weighing up to 300 kg using its trunk.

BUGS

POWER-LIFTING ANTS

Insects are famed for performing amazing feats of strength relative to their small size. Some species of ant can lift around 50 times their own body weight using their powerful mandibles (jaws). If humans were as strong as an ant, they would be able to lift three family cars above their head.

THE MIGHTY DUNG BEETLE

Researchers recently discovered a species of dung beetle called *Onthophagus taurus*, that can pull 1,141 times its own body weight. That's equivalent to a person pulling six double-decker buses full of people. This superhuman strength makes them excellent diggers and dung rollers.

WORLD'S STRONGEST

One of the strongest animals of all is not actually an insect, but species of mite called *Archegozet longisetosus*. It is only 1 mm long but it can hold 1,180 times its weight using its tiny claws. Imagine carrying around nine elephants and you'll have some idea of what this mite can do.

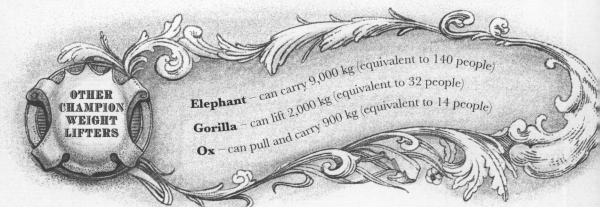

OTHER CHAMPION WEIGHT LIFTERS

Elephant – can carry 9,000 kg (equivalent to 140 people)

Gorilla – can lift 2,000 kg (equivalent to 32 people)

Ox – can pull and carry 900 kg (equivalent to 14 people)

Deathly Grip of the Titanoboa

Slithering through the hot, swampy jungles of South America around 58 million years ago, the 14-metre-long titanoboa was one of the most powerful predators of its day. Like modern boas, it killed its prey by squeezing it to death. Scientists have estimated that it constricted its victims with a force of 28 kg per square cm (kg/cm²) and a total force of up to 600,000 kg – the equivalent of being crushed under the weight of almost 10 tanks!

Powerful Jumpers

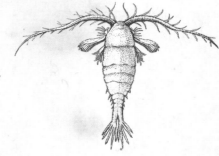

Thanks to their tiny, but extra-powerful, leg muscles, copepods can 'jump' through the water at a speed of 300–1,000 body lengths per second. That's equivalent to a 1.7 m-tall person leaping around 1,700 m in one second.

Winged Creatures

TIGER OF THE SKIES

With its large legs and talons as big as a tiger's claws, the Haast's eagle was one of the most powerful birds that ever lived. It preyed on much bigger flightless birds like the giant moa, crushing the moa's pelvis with its feet. Experts say it may even have been capable of swooping down and killing a small child.

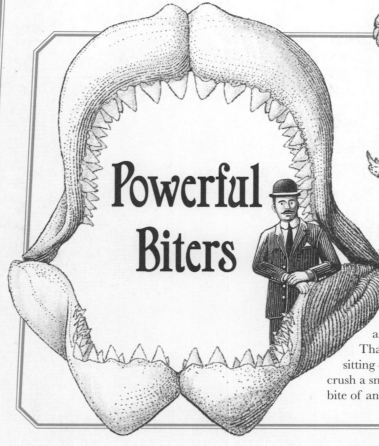

Powerful Biters

With an estimated bite force of more than 5,000 kg, the fearsome T.rex was the most powerful biter of any land animal. But this is nothing compared to the megalodon, which lived in ancient oceans around 16 million years ago. It is thought that these giant sharks could close their jaws around their prey with a force of about 18,100 kg. That's equivalent to four medium-sized elephants sitting down on the ground and powerful enough to crush a small car. The saltwater crocodile has the strongest bite of any animal alive today (around 1,600 kg).

AFRICAN CROWNED EAGLE

One of the strongest birds alive today, the crowned eagle can kill animals more than four times its own body weight.

SNAPPING CLAWS OF THE PISTOL SHRIMP

This feisty crustacean can snap its claws shut with such force that it creates a shockwave that can knock out its prey. The blast is so powerful that some species use it to drill into solid rock and the sound it makes is so loud it can interfere with ships' sonar.

HOW HEAVY?
NATURAL WORLD

OSTRICH EGG
WEIGHT: 1.4 kg

Ostriches lay the largest eggs of all living birds. One egg can weigh as much as 24 chicken eggs (57 g each), or two basketballs (620 g each).

AFRICAN BUSH ELEPHANT
WEIGHT: up to 4.5–6 tonnes

The biggest land mammal – the African bush elephant – weighs the same as around 100 people (with an average weight of 62 kg).

SUMO WRESTLER
WEIGHT: 265 kg

Weighing more than four times the weight of an average person, Ryūichi Yamamoto is thought to be the heaviest Japanese sumo wrestler of all time. Sumo wrestlers reach their gargantuan size by eating vast quantities of chankonabe – a type of Japanese stew.

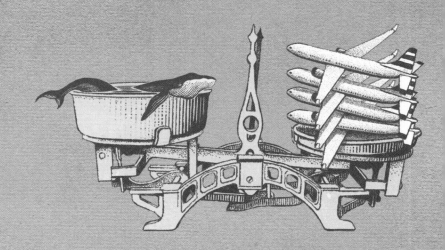

BLUE WHALE
WEIGHT: up to 180 tonnes | tongue: 4 tonnes | heart: 180–680 kg

The heaviest animal on Earth grows to an estimated 180 tonnes – the same as more than four Boeing 737 planes (each weighing about 40 tonnes). Its tongue can weigh as much as an elephant and its heart as much as a small car. It feeds by taking in massive gulps of seawater full of krill, but, despite its size, it can't swallow anything bigger than a beach ball.

CREATURES THEN & NOW

One of the heaviest creatures to have ever stomped the Earth – the Argentinosaurus *– weighed around ten times more than the mighty* T.rex. *The blue whale, however, is around two times heavier than the biggest dinosaurs and weighs more than thirty African elephants.*

Blue whale

Argentinosaurus huinculensis

African bush elephant

Tyrannosaurus rex

Stegosaurus

Southern white rhinoceros

Common hippopotamus

Stegosaurus	Southern white rhinoceros	Common hippopotamus	African bush elephant	Tyrannosaurus rex	Argentinosaurus	Blue whale
3.6 tonnes	3.6 tonnes	3.6 tonnes	6 tonnes	8 tonnes	80 tonnes	180 tonnes

THE WEIGHT OF THE WORLD

cientists have concluded that Earth's mass is approximately

5,972,190,000,000,000,000,000,000 kg.

o, when we build really big things – a skyscraper, an oil
nker or a space rocket – do we make the Earth heavier? The
nswer is no. Humans and things are made with the matter
at is already in the planet. All we're doing is simply moving
oms from one place on the Earth to another.

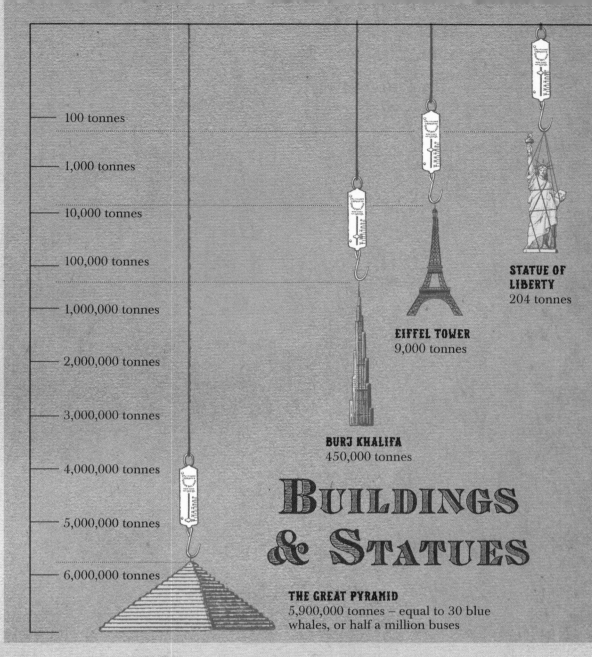

- 100 tonnes
- 1,000 tonnes
- 10,000 tonnes
- 100,000 tonnes
- 1,000,000 tonnes
- 2,000,000 tonnes
- 3,000,000 tonnes
- 4,000,000 tonnes
- 5,000,000 tonnes
- 6,000,000 tonnes

STATUE OF LIBERTY
204 tonnes

EIFFEL TOWER
9,000 tonnes

BURJ KHALIFA
450,000 tonnes

BUILDINGS & STATUES

THE GREAT PYRAMID
5,900,000 tonnes – equal to 30 blue
whales, or half a million buses

PYRAMIDS & MEGALITHS

*Carved from stone hundreds and thousands of years ago, enormous monuments can be found in many
countries around the world. Each giant stone had to be transported – sometimes hundreds of kilometres –
before being heaved into position. Exactly how our ancestors managed to carry out these
amazing engineering feats remains a mystery to this day.*

GREAT PYRAMID OF GIZA, EGYPT
Built: c.2580–2560 BC
Each stone block: 2.5–15 tonnes

STONEHENGE, WILTSHIRE, ENGLAND
Built: c.3000–2500 BC
Heaviest stone: 25–30 tonnes

EASTER ISLAND STATUES, CHILE
Built: c.AD 1100–1600
Heaviest maoi (statue): 74 tonnes

BUSES & SHIPS

The average bus
weighs around
11 tonnes – the
same as about
three hippos.

One of the most famous ships ever
built – RMS *Titanic* – weighed more
than 46,000 tonnes and was the
biggest moveable structure of its day.
Scientists believe the mega-iceberg
that sunk the ship had a mass of
around 1.5 million tonnes.

HUMAN HISTORY *in a week*

If we were to condense all of human history into a **SINGLE WEEK** – with the first *Homo sapiens* arriving in the first second of the first day – the Ancient Egyptian civilization would last just 2.5 hours and Neil Armstrong would take his first steps on the Moon at 2.5 minutes to midnight on the final day...

DAY 7 19:49 — 3000 BC

c.3300 BC
Invention of writing in Sumur, Mesopotamia

c.3000–2500 BC
Stonehenge – a giant stone monument – is built using simple Bronze Age tools.

c.3000–30 BC ANCIENT EGYPTIAN CIVILIZATION

c.3300–600 BC BRONZE AGE
People start using bronze to make tools, weapons, armour and jewellery.

c.3300–1700 BC INDUS VALLEY CIVILIZATION
One of the oldest civilizations. Hinduism probably has its roots in the Indus Valley.

c.4000–330 BC ANCIENT MESOPOTAMIA
One of the earliest great civilization. The first ancient cities are built her

c.2560 BC
The Great Pyramids are built

c.1200–500 BC Start of THE IRON AGE

DAY 7 21:29 — 1000 BC

c.566–410 BC
Life of Buddha and birth of Buddhism

DAY 7 20:39 — 2000 BC

c.1600–1046 BC CHINESE SHANG DYNASTY
The first recorded Chinese dynasty. The earliest examples of Chinese writing are from this period.

c.1100–146 BC ANCIENT GREECE
The Ancient Greeks are famous for being great warriors, poets, politicians and philosophers.

c.776 BC
The first ever Olympic games are held in honour of the Greek god Zeus.

753 BC–AD 476 ANCIENT ROME
At their most powerful, the Romans ruled over much of Europe, North Africa and Asia.

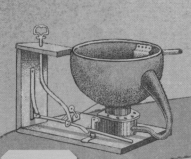

DAY 7 23:34 — AD 1500

DAY 7 23:39 — AD 1600

AD 1596
The first flushing toilet is invented by John Harington.

AD 1532
The Incan Empire is conquered by the conquistador Francisco Pizarro González.

AD 1519–1521 • The mighty Aztec Empire is conquered by Hernán Cortés – a Spanish conquistador (soldier and explorer) – who had come to the Americas in search of gold.

AD 1492
Christopher Columbus accidentally 'discovers' the Americas.

AD 1440
Invention of the printing press by Johannes Gutenberg

AD 1405–1433
The Ming Dynasty admiral Zheng He sails to Asia and Afr bringing back all kinds of exoti objects including pearls, spices, camels, zebras and giraffes.

THE FINAL 10 MINUTES

DAY 7 23:44 — AD 1700

DAY 7 23:49 — AD 1800

AD 1789
French Revolution

AD 1608
Invention of the telescope by Hans Lippershey

AD 1620 • English pilgrims aboard the *Mayflower* arrive at Cape Cod, America.

c.1680–1820 THE AGE OF ENGLIGHTMENT

AD 1776
American Independence

1800s • INDUSTRIAL REVOLUTION
The manufacturing of goods moves from small sho and homes to large factories. Many people move from the countryside to cities, and new technologie and types of transport are introduced.

30

DAY 1
00:00:01

c.200,000 YEARS AGO
First modern humans
(*Homo sapiens*)

DAY 7
16:30
9000 BC

DAY 6
23:00
30,000 BC

DAYS 1–6

c.9000–3300 BC • NEOLITHIC ERA
People begin to live in settlements and learn how to
grow crops. The first animals are domesticated for
their milk, meat and hides. Farming tools, pottery
and weaving are developed.

c.31,000–28,000 BC
Some of the earliest known
examples of rock art

c.200,000–9000 BC
Early humans live a nomadic lifestyle, scavenging or hunting wild
animals like sabre tooth tigers and woolly mammoths. Stone tools
are used for hunting, fishing, building shelters and making clothes.

THE FINAL HOUR

DAY 7
22:19
AD 1

c.AD 570
Birth of Mohammad
and the rise of Islam

206 BC
Invention of
the magnetic
compass
in Ancient
China

c.4 BC–AD 30
Life of Jesus

c.AD 80
Thousands of
gladiators and
animals are killed
in the opening
ceremonies of the
Roman Colosseum.

c.AD 105
Invention of
papermaking
in Ancient
China

c.AD 250–900
MAYAN
CIVILIZATION

c.AD 476–1500
MIDDLE AGES

c.AD 800
Gunpowder is
invented by the
Chinese.

c.AD 800–1050
THE VIKING AGE
The Vikings sail all
over Europe and to
the Americas in their
longboats. Some raid
villages and kill the local
people. Others settle as
farmers, fishermen and
craftsmen.

DAY 7
23:09
AD 1000

DAY 7
23:29
AD 1400

c.AD 1350–1600s
RENAISSANCE
& THE AGE OF
DISCOVERY

DAY 7
23:24
AD 1300

AD 1368–1644
MING DYNASTY
The Chinese Ming finish
the Great Wall and build
a huge palace called the
Forbidden City.

Art, literature and new
ideas about mathematics,
philosophy and science
flourish. Nations explore
the world and discover
new trade routes.

AD 1347–1351
The Black Death kills
around a third of the
population of Europe.

c.AD 1325–1521
AZTEC EMPIRE
A powerful nation
of warriors known
for carrying out
human sacrifices

c.AD 1200–1532 • INCA EMPIRE
The Incas worship the Sun god Inti and
make many beautiful golden objects.
According to legends, the emperor of
Cusco built an entire city with temples,
buildings, plants and trees all made of gold.

DAY 7
23:59
AD 2000

AD 1903 • The world's first
heavier-than-air flying machine

DAY 7
23:54
AD 1900

1885–1886
The first automobile

AD 1914–18
First World War

AD 1939–1945 • Second World
War; the first atomic bomb is
dropped on the city of Hiroshima.

AD 1969
The first man
on the moon

PRESENT DAY
Rovers are sent to Mars
to look for signs of life.

31

History of the Universe

If the whole lifetime of the universe were compressed into a single year, modern humans wouldn't arrive until eight minutes to midnight on the 31 December – the very final day. The past 400 years would pass in the blink of an eye and a single human life would last just a fraction of a second.

The calendar begins with the Big Bang on the 1st of January . . .

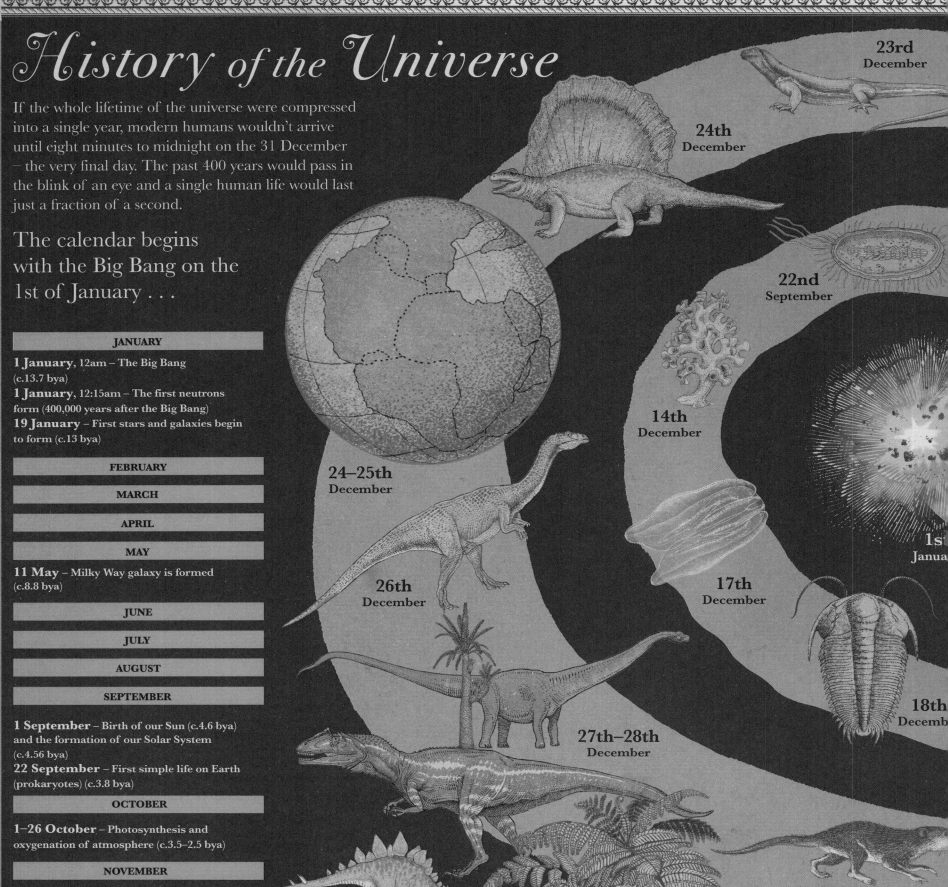

JANUARY

1 January, 12am – The Big Bang (c.13.7 bya)
1 January, 12:15am – The first neutrons form (400,000 years after the Big Bang)
19 January – First stars and galaxies begin to form (c.13 bya)

FEBRUARY
MARCH
APRIL
MAY

11 May – Milky Way galaxy is formed (c.8.8 bya)

JUNE
JULY
AUGUST
SEPTEMBER

1 September – Birth of our Sun (c.4.6 bya) and the formation of our Solar System (c.4.56 bya)
22 September – First simple life on Earth (prokaryotes) (c.3.8 bya)

OCTOBER

1–26 October – Photosynthesis and oxygenation of atmosphere (c.3.5–2.5 bya)

NOVEMBER

9 November – First cells with internal organs develop on Earth (c.2 bya)

DECEMBER

11–17 December – First multicellular life and simple animals: sponges, jellyfish, sea anemones and corals (c.800–580 mya)
18 December – First vertebrates (creatures with back bones) and trilobites, the first hard-bodied animals (c.520 mya)
19 December – First non-vascular land plants (without roots, stems or leaves) (c.470 mya) and first insects (c.479 mya)
20 December – First vascular plants (c.430 mya) and first fish with jaws, such as *Entelognathus* (c.419 mya)
21 December – First flying insects (c.400 mya) and first trees (c.380 mya). As plants grow taller, insects develop flight. By 300 million years ago, there are species of damselflies as big as a seagull.
22 December – First amphibians (c.360 mya). Animals develop adaptations for living on land as well as in water.
23 December – First reptiles (c.312 mya). Animals, such as the lizard-like *Hylonomus*, evolve to live entirely on dry land.
24 December – Mammal-like reptiles, such as the bizarre-looking *Edaphosaurus*, begin to thrive on land. They have clawed feet, sharp teeth, and large sails on their back (c.300–288 mya).
24–25 December – The continents join together in a supercontinent called Pangaea, allowing animals to roam more freely (c.299–272 mya)
26 December – The first dinosaurs evolve from reptiles (c.230 mya). Early types include the plant-eating *Plateosaurus*.
27–28 December – Jurassic period (c.201–145 mya). The high point of the dinosaurs. Species include *Allosaurus*, *Stegosaurus* and *Diplodocus*.
27 December – First 'true' mammals (c.160 mya). The earliest known placental mammals, such as the *Juramaia*, are small and shrew-like.
28 December – First birds evolve from small carnivorous dinosaurs (c.150 mya)
28–30 December – Cretaceous period (c.145–66 mya). The age of the giant dinosaurs and pterosaurs continues – including *Tyrannosaurus*, *Argentinosaurus*, *Triceratops*, *Iguanodon* and *Quetzalcoatlus*.
28 December – First flowers (c.130 mya). Thought to be one of the most important

On this scale:
Each day = 37.5 million years
Each hour = 1.56 million years
Each minute = 26,000 years
Each second = 434 years

...oments in the history of life on Earth. ...een forests become filled with colour, ...d new species of insects, birds and ...imals flourish.

... **December** – At 00:01 a huge ...teroid or comet collides with Earth ...using the mass extinction of 65–75 ...r cent of all species, including all ...n-bird dinosaurs and marine reptiles. ...66 mya). Mammals diversify and at ...out 16:00 the first mammals – such as ...e *Ambulocetus* (or 'walking whale') – take ...the seas (c.50 mya).

THE FINAL DAY – 31 December
Mammals continue to diversify on land and at sea, and reach enormous sizes (giraffes, mammoths, whales).

18:54 – Expansion of grasslands around the world (c.8–3 mya)
20:10 – First human-like apes (c.6 mya)
21:26 – Early hominids first walk upright on two legs (c.4 mya)
22:24 – Ice Age begins, first use of stone tools, rise of megafauna (c.2.5 mya)
23:52 – *Homo sapiens* (c.200,000 ya)

23.57 – Human migration around the world (c.80,000 ya)
23.59 – Early cave paintings (c.33,000 ya)

THE FINAL MINUTE
23:59:33 – End of Ice Age (c.11,600 ya)
23:59:33 – Farming begins (c.10,000 ya)
23:59:45 – Wheel invented (c.5,500 ya)
23:59:48 – Stonehenge built (c.5,000 ya)
23:59:49 – Great Pyramids (c.4,500 ya)
23:59:55 – Colosseum built (c.2,000 ya)
23:59:58 – Columbus sails to the Americas (c.525 ya)

THE FINAL SECOND
In the final second humankind has invented the telescope, the microscope and the first flushing toilet. We have built palaces and skyscrapers; discovered penicillin and cured diseases; invented cars, trains, planes, the telephone and the internet. We have had revolutions and wars, dropped the first atomic bomb, put a man on the Moon and sent probes to the planet Mars!

ya = years ago • mya = million years ago • bya = billion years ago

33

SMALL CREATURES

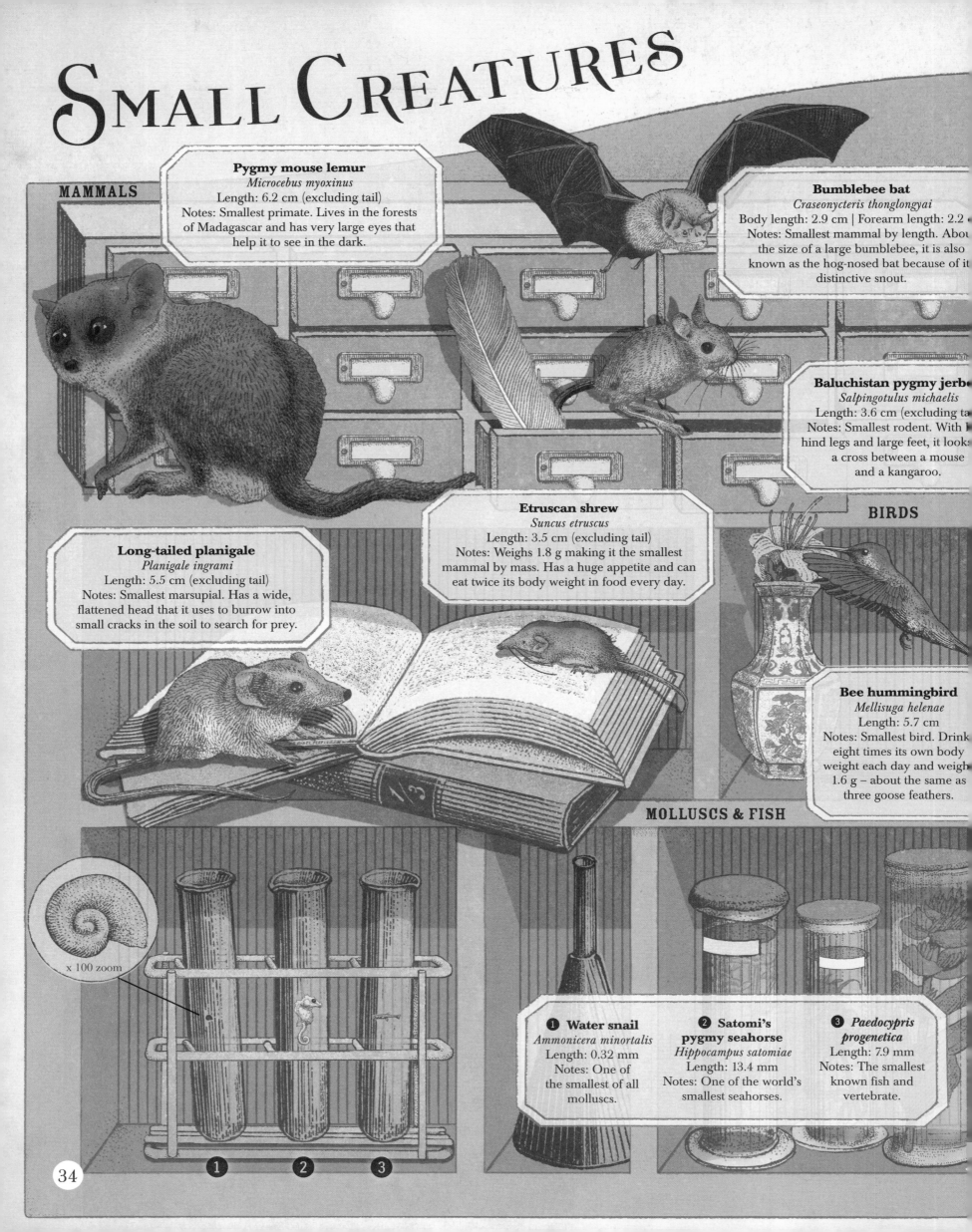

MAMMALS

Pygmy mouse lemur
Microcebus myoxinus
Length: 6.2 cm (excluding tail)
Notes: Smallest primate. Lives in the forests of Madagascar and has very large eyes that help it to see in the dark.

Bumblebee bat
Craseonycteris thonglongyai
Body length: 2.9 cm | Forearm length: 2.2
Notes: Smallest mammal by length. Abou
the size of a large bumblebee, it is also
known as the hog-nosed bat because of it
distinctive snout.

Baluchistan pygmy jerb
Salpingotulus michaelis
Length: 3.6 cm (excluding ta
Notes: Smallest rodent. With
hind legs and large feet, it looks
a cross between a mouse
and a kangaroo.

Etruscan shrew
Suncus etruscus
Length: 3.5 cm (excluding tail)
Notes: Weighs 1.8 g making it the smallest
mammal by mass. Has a huge appetite and can
eat twice its body weight in food every day.

Long-tailed planigale
Planigale ingrami
Length: 5.5 cm (excluding tail)
Notes: Smallest marsupial. Has a wide,
flattened head that it uses to burrow into
small cracks in the soil to search for prey.

BIRDS

Bee hummingbird
Mellisuga helenae
Length: 5.7 cm
Notes: Smallest bird. Drink
eight times its own body
weight each day and weigh
1.6 g – about the same as
three goose feathers.

MOLLUSCS & FISH

x 100 zoom

❶ **Water snail**
Ammonicera minortalis
Length: 0.32 mm
Notes: One of
the smallest of all
molluscs.

❷ **Satomi's
pygmy seahorse**
Hippocampus satomiae
Length: 13.4 mm
Notes: One of the world's
smallest seahorses.

❸ *Paedocypris
progenetica*
Length: 7.9 mm
Notes: The smallest
known fish and
vertebrate.

34

PTILES, AMPHIBIANS & BUTTERFLIES

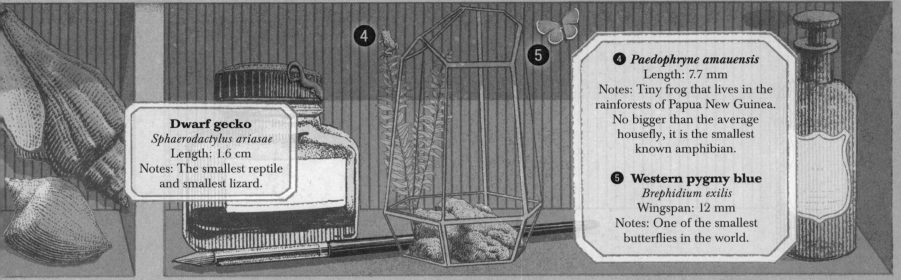

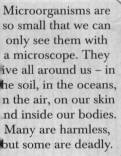

Dwarf gecko
Sphaerodactylus ariasae
Length: 1.6 cm
Notes: The smallest reptile
and smallest lizard.

④ *Paedophryne amauensis*
Length: 7.7 mm
Notes: Tiny frog that lives in the
rainforests of Papua New Guinea.
No bigger than the average
housefly, it is the smallest
known amphibian.

⑤ Western pygmy blue
Brephidium exilis
Wingspan: 12 mm
Notes: One of the smallest
butterflies in the world.

MICROORGANISMS

Microorganisms are
so small that we can
only see them with
a microscope. They
live all around us – in
the soil, in the oceans,
n the air, on our skin
nd inside our bodies.
Many are harmless,
but some are deadly.

⑥ Fairyfly *or* Fairywasp
Dicopomorpha echmepterygis
Length: 139 microns (0.139 mm)
Notes: Parasitic wasp that lives
inside the eggs of other insects.
Smallest known insect.

Diatoms (various species)
Length: Typically between 2–500 microns (0.002–0.5 mm)
Notes: Microscopic algae that live in nearly every habitat where water is
found. They are eaten by all kinds of animals from tiny microorganisms to
fish and whales. Hundreds of them could fit on a single grain of sand.

⑦ *Pelagibacter ubique*
Length: 0.37–0.89 microns
(0.00037–0.00089 mm)
tes: One of the smallest free-living
cterium. More than 5,000 of them
ould fit on a single grain of sand.

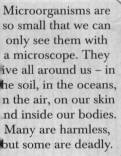

x 100 zoom

⑥

⑦

x 50,000
zoom

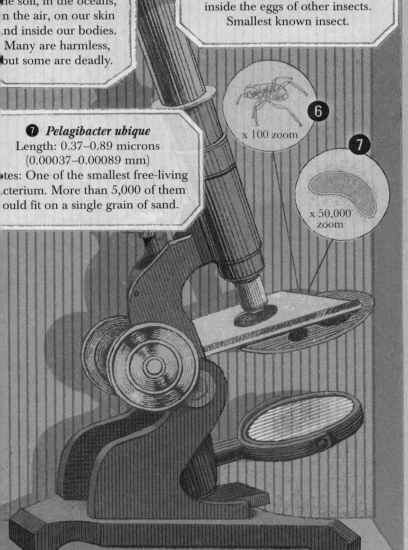

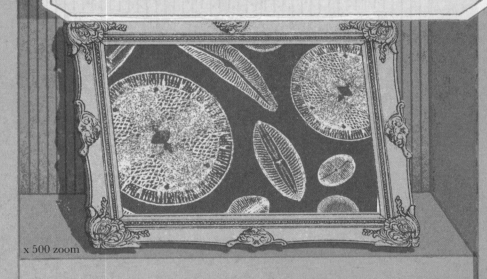

x 500 zoom

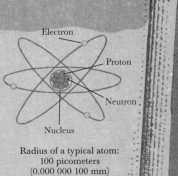

HOW SMALL IS AN ATOM?
Everything in the universe – from
the tallest tower to the smallest
microorganism – is made up of tiny
things called atoms. They are the
building blocks of all matter and they
are very, very small. They are around a
million times smaller than the thickest
human hair and are so small that if the
atoms in an apple were enlarged to
the size of an apple, the apple itself
would be as big as the Earth.

Electron

Proton

Neutron

Nucleus

Radius of a typical atom:
100 picometers
(0.000 000 100 mm)

Stars AND Galaxies

STARS

Stars come in all different sizes and colours, from red dwarfs and neutron stars to blue and red supergiants – the biggest stars in the universe. Our star – the Sun – is at the centre of our Solar System. Without its heat and light, no life could survive on Earth.

Giant Stars

Our Sun is the largest object in our Solar System, but compared to some stars it is no bigger than a fleck of dust. The biggest stars in the universe are the monster red supergiants – dying stars that have bloated to many times their original size. Eventually they will explode and become neutron stars or black holes.

Smallest Stars

(The numbers in brackets show the solar radii. 1R = Radius of the Sun)

Sun
(main sequence star)
Radius: 695,700 km
Our Sun is a main sequence star –
one of the most common types of star.
It is fuelled through 'nuclear fusion';
as its hydrogen atoms crash together
they become helium and
produce energy.

Sun

Rigel
(blue supergiant)
Radius: 54,290,000 km (78R)
Blue supergiants are the hottest and
brightest stars in the universe. Rigel
is more than 70 times bigger than
the Sun and emits 60,000 times
more light.

Pollux
(red giant)
Radius:
6,122,160 (8.8 R)
As a star like our
Sun runs out of fue
it grows bigger and
redder, turning into
red giant. Eventual
it will collapse and
become a white dw

Rigel

2MASS Jo523-1403
(red dwarf star)
Radius: 59,830 km (0.086 R)
Red dwarfs are main
sequence stars like our Sun,
but are smaller and cooler.

Jupiter
Radius: 69,911 km (0.1 R)
The biggest planet in our
Solar System

Around the Earth
on a rocket: 1 hour

Earth
Radius: 6,371 km
(0.009 R)

Betelgeuse
(red supergiant)
Radius: 820,926,000 km (1,180 R)
This supergiant is more than
a thousand times wider than
our Sun.

Neutron star
(Not visible on this scale)
Measuring as little as 20 km
across, neutron stars are the
smallest stars known to exist.

Sirius B (white dwarf star)
Radius: 5,844 km (0.0084 R)
As an average star like
our Sun dies, it becomes a
white dwarf – a small, hot
and very dense star.

UY Scuti
(red supergiant)
Radius: 1,182,690,000 km (1,700 R)
The biggest known star by radius is more than
1,700 times the size of the Sun. If Earth were
shrunk to the size of a marble, the Sun would
be the size of a child and UY Scuti would be
taller than two Burj Khalifas.

Death of a Star

As a massive star nears the end of its life it explodes as a supernova – an explosion so big that it briefly shines more brightly than an entire galaxy.

A star that is born 8–20 times more massive than the Sun ends its life as a neutron star.

As it explodes, the star's core is squashed down into a tiny compact ball known as a neutron star. It is so dense that one cubic cm might weigh around a billion tonnes. That's the mass of Mt Everest, but squeezed into a space the size of a sugar cube.

A star that is born at least 20 times more massive than the Sun ends its life as a black hole.

The star's core is compressed into a space no bigger than an atom and its gravitational pull is so strong that nothing can escape it – not even light.

To the Edge of the Universe

Scientists have estimated that the observable universe – in other words the part that we can see – has a diameter of 93 billion light years. Our Milky Way would fit inside it 10 million million million (10,000,000,000,000,000,000) times.

Across the known universe on a rocket: 2.5 quadrillion (2,510,981,500,000,000) years

How Big is the Universe?

So how big is the entire universe? No one really knows if the universe stretches on forever, or even if ours is the only universe that exists.

GALAXIES

Until a hundred or so years ago, few people imagined that anything existed beyond our galaxy – the Milky Way. We now know that it is just one of billions of galaxies in the universe. Some are very small. Others are much, much bigger than our own.

Galaxies Compared

Messier 33
(spiral galaxy)
Diameter:
50,000 light years

Milky Way
(spiral galaxy)
Diameter:
100,000 light years
There are around
200 billion stars in
the Milky Way.

Across the Milky Way on a rocket: 2.7 billion (2,699,980,022.8) years

Andromeda
(spiral galaxy)
Diameter: 220,000 light years
Our nearest galaxy. Andromeda is expected to collide with the Milky Way in around 4.6 billion years to form a giant elliptical galaxy.

Milky Way

IC11-01
(super giant elliptical galaxy)
Diameter: 6,000,000 light years
Over billions of years, galaxies like our Milky Way have collided and merged together to form this super galaxy. It is around 50 times wider than the Milky Way and may contain as many as 100 trillion stars. At its centre is a supermassive black hole.